TIME FOR KIDS

UNSOLVED!

History's Mysteries

Dona Herweck Rice

Consultants

Timothy Rasinski, Ph.D.
Kent State University

Lori Oczkus
Literacy Consultant

Publishing Credits

Dona Herweck Rice, *Editor-in-Chief*
Lee Aucoin, *Creative Director*
Jamey Acosta, *Senior Editor*
Heidi Fiedler, *Editor*
Lexa Hoang, *Designer*
Stephanie Reid, *Photo Editor*
Rane Anderson, *Contributing Author*
Rachelle Cracchiolo, *M.S.Ed., Publisher*

Image Credits: pp.19 (top), 23 (lower middle) Alamy; p.25 Corbis; p.48 Dona Rice; pp.11, 15 (left), 16 (middle & bottom), 23 (upper middle), 28 (right middle), 30, 33 (top right), 35 (bottom) Getty Images; cover & pp.5, 12 (bottom), 26 (bottom), 29 (top), 34, 40–41, 48 (bottom) iStockphoto; p.7 (bottom) Library of Congress [LC-USZ62-10187]; p.22 (top) Library of Congress [LC-DIG-pga-02388]; p.31 (bottom) Library of Congress [LC-DIG-npcc-25207]; pp.20–21 NASA; p.18 (bottom) akg-images/British Library/ Newscom; p.23 (bottom) akg-images/Newscom; p.35 (top) Danita Delimont/Newscom; p.29 (bottom) EPA/Hugo Philpott/Newscom; p.13 (top) NASA/Newscom; pp. 32–33 Picture History/ Newscom; p.9 (right) REUTERS/Newscom; p.7 (top) Richard Chamberlanin/Newscom; p.10 UPI/ Newscom; p.13 (bottom) ZUMA Press/Newscom; pp.23 (top), 37 (middle) Photo Researchers Inc.; p.32 (left) The Bridgeman Art Library; pp.17, 28 (left) The Granger Collection; All other images from Shutterstock.

Teacher Created Materials
5301 Oceanus Drive
Huntington Beach, CA 92649-1030
http://www.tcmpub.com

ISBN 978-1-4333-4829-7

Printed by: 51497
Printed in: China

Table of Contents

For Real?

Oh, come on! Is that real? You will wonder that and more when you read about the strange disappearances, larger-than-life creatures, and mysterious happenings in this book. Are they real? What happened? Only history knows for sure. Could anything like that happen again? Perhaps that's a mystery for another time . . . .

THINK LINK

History is more than the facts in a book. But there are some things we may never understand. And the truth is, some of the most famous events in history are also some of the most mysterious.

- How could some of history's most famous figures disappear?
- Did some of history's biggest moments really happen?
- Is there another side to these stories we don't know yet?

Whatever Happened To?

It's hard to do anything without being watched! Cameras are everywhere. They are posted on buildings. People have camera phones ready to film what they see. You would be surprised how many times *you* appear on film each day!

But it wasn't always this way. There were times when people came and went without video records. And even now, people who want to disappear—or make others disappear—can figure out a way.

Masked Prisoner

From around 1669 until his death in 1703, a mysterious man was held in jails throughout France. Most of the time he was in the **Bastille** (ba-STEEL). No one ever saw the man's face. It was always covered with a black velvet mask. The prisoner's name was Eustache Dauger (YOO-stay-sh DOH-zhay). That is probably not his real name. Dauger was told that if he talked about himself, he would be killed. Only the head of the Bastille was allowed to see his face. No one knows who he was or why he was jailed.

At least a dozen movies have been made about the mysterious prisoner. They usually show him in a mask made of iron.

The True King?

Many people believe the prisoner was the brother of King Louis XIV—maybe even a twin brother. They think he was jailed by Louis XIV so no one could stop Louis from being the king.

The Bastille was a huge fortress used mainly as a prison by the royal leaders of France.

D.B. Cooper

On November 24, 1971, a man entered a Portland airport. He called himself Dan Cooper. That day, he bought a ticket to Seattle. After takeoff, Cooper handed a note to the flight attendant. It read, "You are being **hijacked**." He wanted money, parachutes, and more fuel. The **Federal Bureau of Investigation (FBI)** gathered the ransom. The plane circled above. Two hours later, the plane landed in Seattle. Cooper let most people off. He got the **ransom** money and four parachutes. The plane refueled and took off again. Cooper had the pilot fly low and head south. Then, Cooper jumped out of the plane! He was gone. No one knows what his real name was. The FBI isn't sure if he is dead. They are still looking for him.

This is the only unsolved airplane hijacking in all of American flight history.

Who Was D.B.?

A small-time criminal in the Portland area was named D.B. Cooper. The FBI thought maybe he was Dan Cooper. But they were wrong. The newspapers found out about this and printed that Dan Cooper was D.B. Cooper anyway. That name has stuck ever since.

Jimmy Hoffa

Jimmy Hoffa was a union boss from 1932 to 1975. He led the **Teamsters**, one of the most powerful **unions** of the time. But Hoffa didn't always play nice. He may have worked with organized crime.

On July 30, 1975, Hoffa was supposed to meet two men at a Detroit restaurant. Hoffa was nervous. One of the men was a big crime boss. When the men didn't show, Hoffa called his wife. He said he had been stood up. Hoffa never came home. A truck driver said he had seen Hoffa in the backseat of a car that nearly hit his truck coming out of the parking lot.

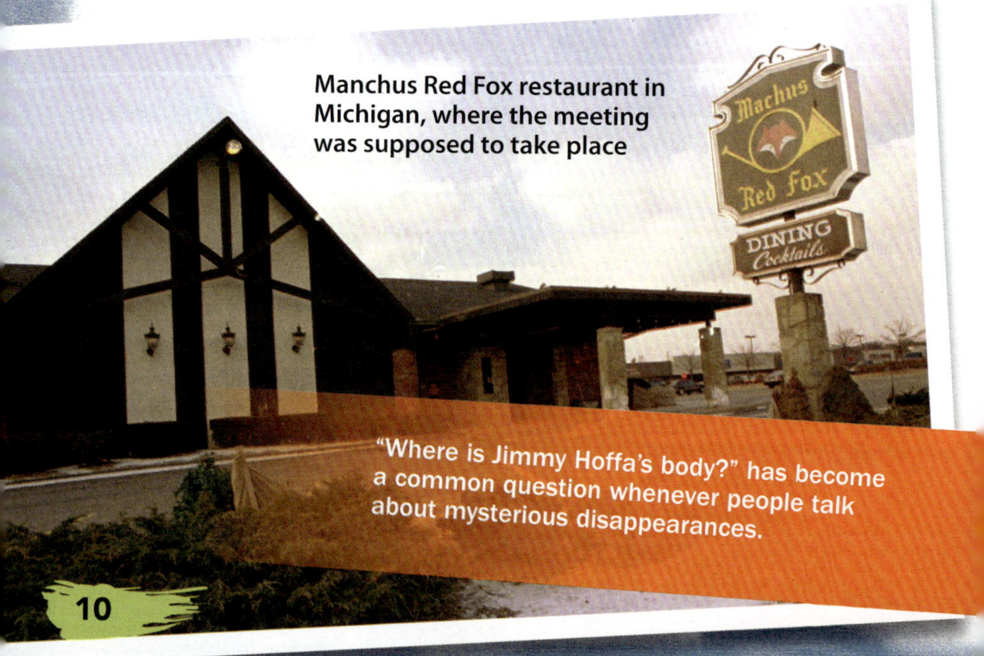

Manchus Red Fox restaurant in Michigan, where the meeting was supposed to take place

"Where is Jimmy Hoffa's body?" has become a common question whenever people talk about mysterious disappearances.

Jimmy Hoffa

The car was **traced** to a man whom Hoffa had helped care for. Police dogs found Hoffa's scent in the trunk of the car. But everyone had an **alibi** (AL-uh-bahy).

Police never found a body. They feel sure they know who killed Hoffa. And they know why. They just don't know what happened to Hoffa. And they don't know where his body is.

Organized Crime

The FBI defines organized crime as crime committed by a group with a formal structure. The group's primary purpose is to make money through illegal activities. Many of these groups use violence or threats to control the people in their community.

Amelia Earhart

In the early days of plane travel, very few women flew planes. Amelia Earhart was one of the first. In 1932, she was the first woman to cross the Atlantic Ocean solo. And she tried to circle the globe in 1937. But during the flight, radio contact was lost. She was near an island where she was supposed to land. The last thing anyone heard from her was "We must be on you, but we cannot see you. Fuel is running low. . . ." All was silent after that. Earhart and her plane were never found.

Alive?

There are many people who think that perhaps Earhart crashed on a remote island and survived. Even if this were true, she would long since have died. But stories of her survival continue.

On her attempt to circle the globe, Earhart's last stop for fuel was Lae, New Guinea. People there were the last to see her.

I Saw Elvis

When a famous person dies young, tragically, or in a mysterious way, there seem to be countless people who don't really believe the person died. Stories pop up everywhere of people who insist they have seen the person alive and well. The rock-and-roll superstar Elvis Presley is one example of this. He died in 1977, but people today still say they have spotted him.

Vanishing Act

The Bermuda Triangle is a place where dozens of boats, planes, and people have vanished. It is located in the Atlantic Ocean. Some people think this area is very dangerous. They think there is a magnetic field there that causes compasses to stop working. Others think the strong water currents and weather conditions are the reason for the disappearances.

Without a Trace

In 1918, a U.S. Naval ship went missing after leaving the island of Barbados and traveling into the Bermuda Triangle. The ship and crew of 306 people vanished without a trace. Some people blame storms or a wartime enemy. Others say there would be **remains** of the ship or the crew if the disappearance had been due to a storm or wartime combat.

Flight 19

In 1945, five U.S. Navy bombers flew out of Fort Lauderdale, Florida, on a training flight. The pilots became lost within the Bermuda Triangle. Through one of the plane's radios, the leader of the group said his compass was off. He also said everything looked strange, and he couldn't figure out where they were. A sixth plane that was sent out to find them also vanished. And although the Navy called for all planes and boats in the area to look out for them, no trace of the planes was ever found.

Anastasia

Nicholas Romanov's family was killed in 1918.

There was big trouble in Russia in the early 1900s. The people wanted to get rid of the old rulers. Nicholas II was the current ruler. He was married and had five children. Anastasia Romanov was his youngest daughter.

On July 17, 1918, the secret police killed Nicholas and his family. But did Anastasia survive?

the Romanovs

"All the News That's Fit to Print."

The New York Times.

NEW YORK, FRIDAY, MARCH 16, 1917.—TWENTY PAGES.

VOLUTION IN RUSSIA; CZAR ABDICATES
ICHAEL MADE REGENT, EMPRESS IN HIDIN
RO-GERMAN MINISTERS REPORTED SL

LONDON HAILS REVOLUTION

Expected Czar's Overthrow and Sees Brighter Prospects for the Allies.

THINK THE COUP DECISIVE

Duma Appeals to the Army for Unity Against Foe; Gives Pledge of No Weakening or Suspension of War

ARMY JOINS WITH THE DUMA

Three Days of Conflict Follow Food Riots in Capital.

POPULACE TAKE UP ARMS

But End Comes Suddenly When Troops Guarding Old Ministers Surrender.

FEAR NO SEPARATE PEACE

FRYATT'S FATE

For years, many people thought so. Several women claimed they were the lost **duchess**. They stepped forward to claim the family fortune. But in 2009, science proved them all wrong. It is certain that the whole family died that day.

Anastasia, age 9

Anna

Anna Anderson is the most famous person to claim she was Anastasia. Many movies, books, and plays have been written about her story. But now, we know that all of them are false. Decades after the **czar's** death, the location of his body and that of his wife and children was finally found. **DNA tests** confirmed their identities. They compared Anna Anderson's DNA with Anastasia's remains, but they did not match.

Who Was Jack the Ripper?

One of the most famous criminals in history is known as Jack the Ripper. In 1888, he murdered several poor women in London. He was never caught. Today, there are more than 100 theories about who he was. But the case has never been solved.

Dear Boss

After the murders, a mysterious letter surfaced, written by a person claiming to be the murderer. The author promised to cut the ear of his next victim. Three days later, another murder took place. The murder victim's ear was partially nicked. Was it just a coincidence?

Police searched for Jack the Ripper but never made an arrest.

Dear Boss,
I keep on hearing the police have caught me but they won't fix me just yet. I have laughed when they look so clever and talk about being on the right track...
—Jack the Ripper

What's in a Name?

The murderer signed the letter "Jack the Ripper." Many people believe the letter was a **hoax**. But the name seemed to stick. People are still calling him Jack the Ripper.

Can We Believe It?

Grainy images on TV show something unbelievable. A flash of something large and hairy darts through the forest. A serpent-like shadow arches over the water and then is gone. A poor man with little education creates the greatest plays of all time. Can any of this be real?

Thirteen percent of people who took a survey in 1988 believed the moon is made of cheese!

The spaceflight *Apollo 11* only had 20 seconds of fuel left before it landed safely on the moon.

Moon Landing

As an amazed world watched, the first people landed on the moon on July 20, 1969. People watched the event on their small TVs. They could hardly believe the men had landed safely and stepped on the moon's rocky surface.

To this day, not everyone believes they really did. In fact, some don't think people have *ever* landed on the moon! They insist that everything was done on a movie set.

Columbus Discovers America

For years, schools have taught that Christopher Columbus found America. But is it true? In 1492, Columbus sailed from Europe with three ships. He was looking for riches in the Indies. Instead, he landed on an island near Florida. But there were already people there. So, some people say Columbus didn't really discover America. Historians still argue about who first came to the New World.

New to You

One reason historians give credit to Columbus is that before his voyages, America was still mostly unknown to the world. After Columbus, knowledge of the "New World" became widespread.

Early Explorers

His name may be famous, but Columbus was not the first to arrive in America.

13,000 BC

Historians have discovered remains that show the first humans may have arrived in North America more than 15,000 years ago.

AD 1000

Five hundred years before Columbus, Viking Leif Erikson sailed with 35 men to the island of Newfoundland off the coast of Canada.

AD 1422

Others believe the Chinese traveled to the Americas 70 years before Columbus.

AD 1492

In 1492, Columbus discovered a small island off the coast of the Americas. Thousands of people were already living there when he arrived, but he claimed the land for Spain.

Bigfoot

Many people in the Pacific Northwest claimed to have seen a giant apelike wild man. They say he roams through the forest. He walks upright, is more than seven feet tall, and has huge feet, they claim. Some people have taken photos, but no one can tell for sure if it is a real creature or just a person in an ape suit! Some scientists think bigfoot may be real.

On the Trail

Bigfoot is known by many different names. But each name describes a similar large apelike creature roaming nearby woods and forests.

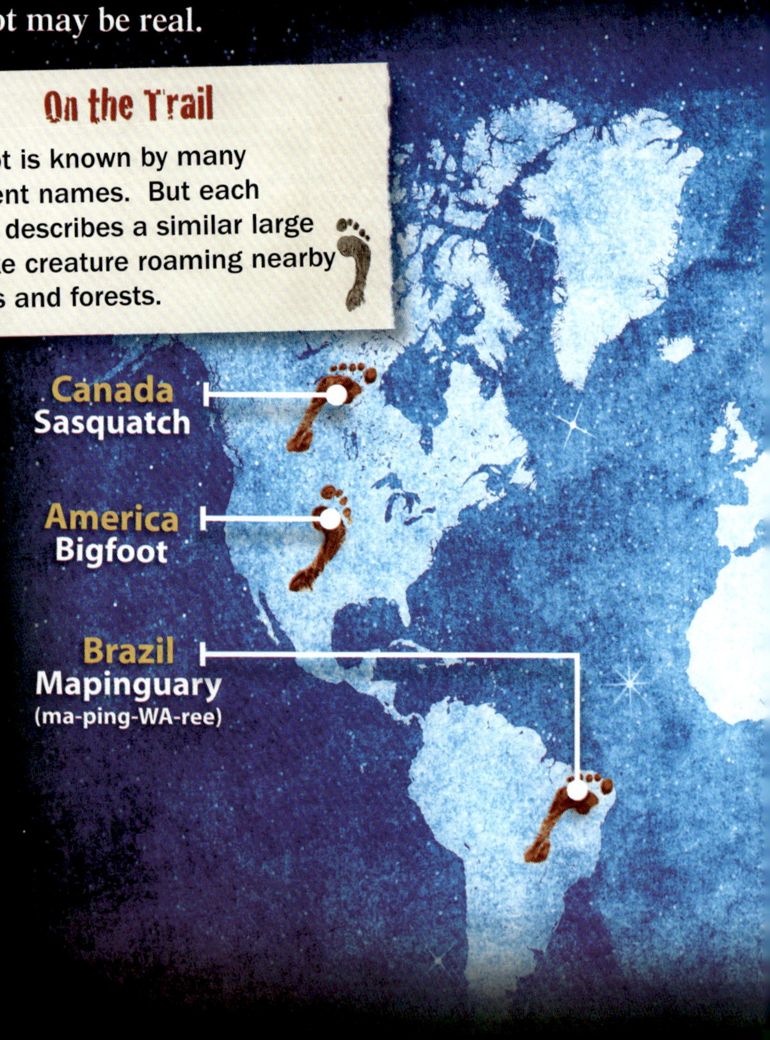

First Reports

Bigfoot is also called *Sasquatch* (SAS-kwoch), which comes from the Salish Indian word *sésquac*, meaning "wild man." Stories of wild men were told among the native people of the Pacific Northwest for centuries. The stories were first written in the 1920s by J.W. Burns. He was also the first to call the creature *Sasquatch*.

This famous photo has led some to believe Bigfoot is real.

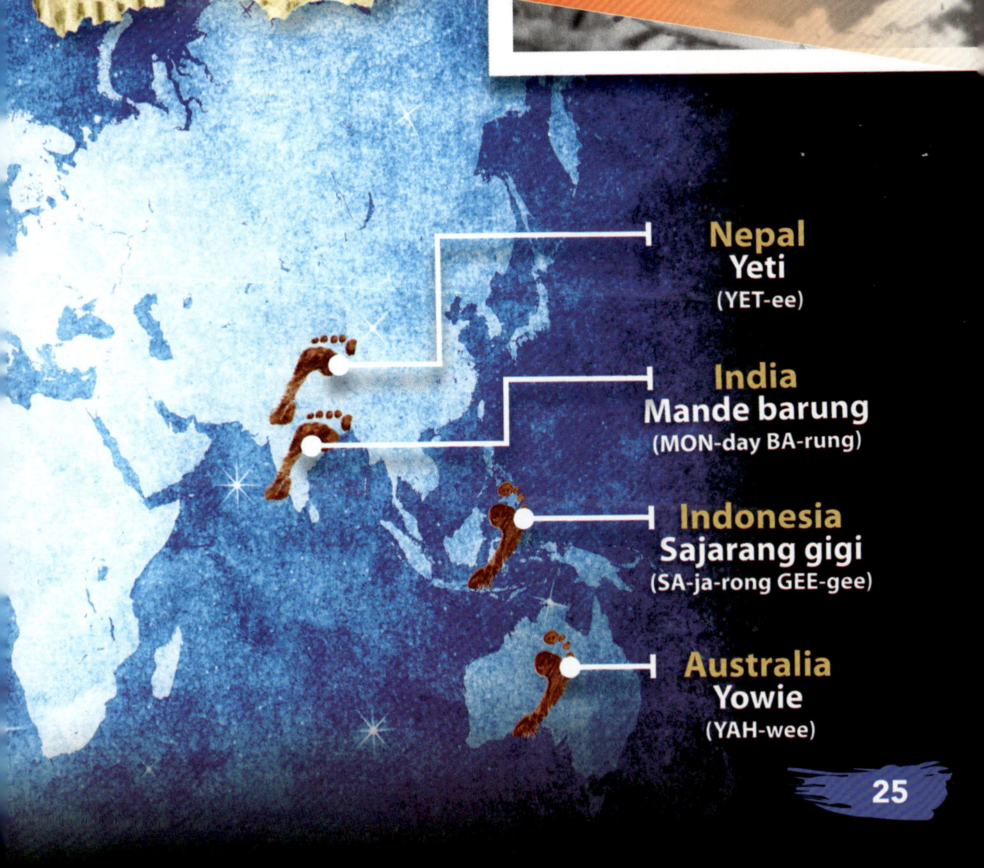

The Loch Ness Monster

One of the most famous places in Scotland is Loch Ness. People say a giant sea monster lives there! They believe it lives mainly underwater. But now and then, people are sure they see it rise above the surface. When they look for it, no one finds real evidence that the creature exists. But the stories continue. People can't explain the strange things they see.

The photographer of this famous 1934 photo claims it shows the head and neck of the Loch Ness monster.

In 1976, an attempt was made to lure Nessie to the surface of the water with bacon. Why bacon? Who knows? But it didn't work.

Deep Truths

The Loch Ness monster was first reported by an Irish monk in the seventh century. Coming upon the burial of a man in the Loch Ness area, he asked how the man died. The people said he was killed by a giant water beast. They said it attacked the man while he was swimming.

Shakespeare

Many people say that William Shakespeare wrote the greatest plays and poetry in history. The Bard, as he is called, lived in 16th century England. He came from a working family. Most poor people had no education. And he only had a little. Yet his work is **genius**. It is filled with details that only a very educated person would know. It's for this reason many people believe Shakespeare really didn't write his works.

The Usual Suspects

If Shakespeare didn't write his works, who did? The most popular answers include Christopher Marlowe, Francis Bacon, and Edward de Vere. They were all well-educated and brilliant men of the time. Some people say they were written by Queen Elizabeth I.

▲ Christopher Marlowe

▲ Francis Bacon

▲ Edward de Vere

▲ Queen Elizabeth I

The Final Word

These words are inscribed on Shakespeare's tombstone:

Curst be he that moves my bones.

What's the Real Story?

Whole civilizations have vanished. And whole communities have seemed to go mad. All this occurred without any real explanation. What happened to these people? We may never know for sure. But that doesn't keep us from wondering!

Roanoke

In the 16th century, England tried to set up a colony in the New World. They called it Roanoke (ROH-uh-nokh). Supplies were given to the colony for a while. But the organizers were not able to return to the colony for three years. During that time, all the people disappeared. There were no signs of struggle or war. The people had just vanished.

Sir Walter Raleigh organized Roanoke Colony. Many years passed before he tried to discover what happened to the colony. He never found the answer.

Dare to Believe

The Dare Stones are a collection of 48 hand-carved stones. Each stone offers a clue about what might have happened to the lost colony. **Allegedly** written by Eleanor Dare, a Roanoke settler, the stones tell what became of the colony. Most historians believe the stones are fakes.

Salem Witch Trials

In 1692 in Salem, hundreds of people were accused of witchcraft. Some young women and political leaders started the madness. Twenty were killed, and four died in prison.

How did this happen? A strange combination of reasons might have caused the witch trials. Some say it was teenage boredom. Some say it was family feuds. Some say it was money. Whatever the reasons, fear took over. When the madness stopped, many couldn't believe what they had done.

Even two dogs were killed as helpers to the witches!

The accused were hanged in public.

The Accused: 1692

June 10
Bridget Bishop

July 19
Sarah Good
Elizabeth Howe
Susannah Martin
Rebecca Nurse
Sarah Wildes

August 19
George Burroughs
Martha Carrier
George Jacobs Sr.
John Proctor
John Willard

September 19
Giles Corey

September 22
Martha Corey
Mary Eastey
Ann Pudeator
Alice Parker
Mary Parker
Wilmott Redd
Margaret Scott
Samuel Wardwell

Mayan Empire

The Mayan Empire was one of the greatest in history. It thrived from 2,600 BC until AD 900. Then, it quickly disappeared. Why?

People think there may have been disasters such as earthquakes. Or maybe there was a revolt by the poor. Maybe disease took over. Maybe all the **resources** were used up and people couldn't survive anymore. The truth? No one really knows.

The Mayan people built amazing structures including this temple. ▶

Anasazi

Like the Maya, the Anasazi (ah-nuh-SAH-zee) disappeared. They were the dominant culture for hundreds of years in the American southwest, beginning around AD 900. But they disappeared suddenly. The most likely reasons are climate changes, drought, or warring enemies.

The Anasazi lived in amazing cliff-side structures.

Spiritual leaders were a large part of Mayan culture.

The Neanderthals

Neanderthals (nee-AN-der-thawlz) lived over 50,000 years ago. At that time, modern humans were spreading out across Earth. Today, only humans survive. Neanderthals are now **extinct**.

Scientists study Neanderthal bones to learn about them. We know they were like humans in some ways. But they had shorter arms and legs, heavy jaws, and strong muscles. No one is sure why they didn't survive.

Where Did They Go?

People have speculated that modern man fought with the Neanderthals until they were no longer able to survive. Today, some scientists think they had trouble adapting when the climate became warmer and dryer. Others think Neanderthals didn't have enough children to survive.

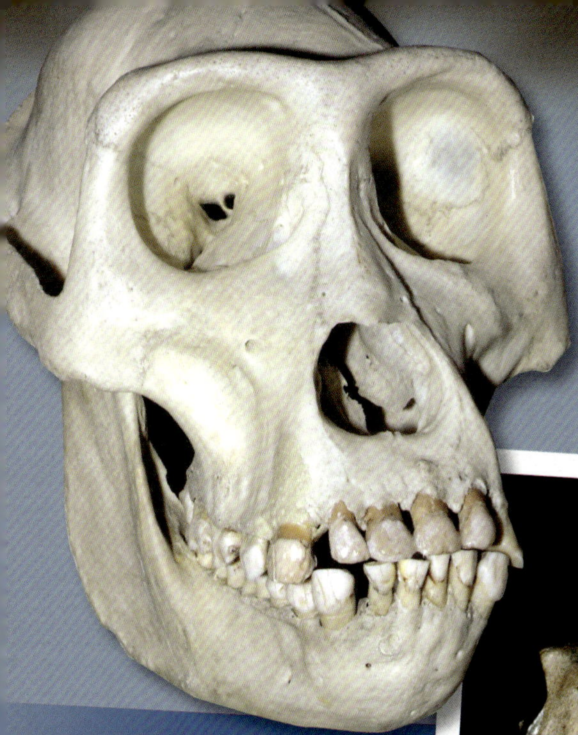

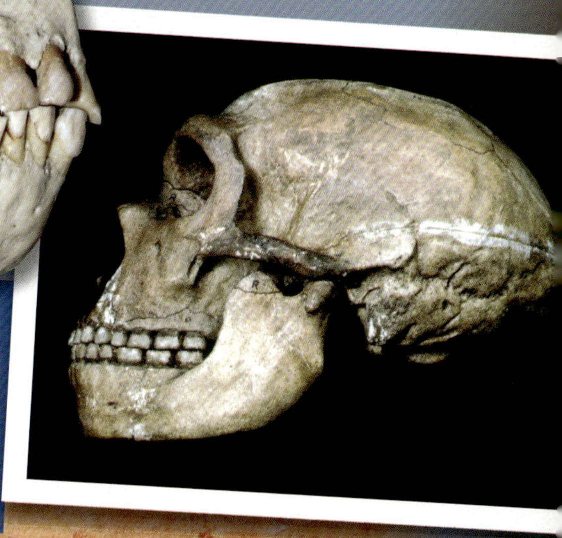

The first discovery of Neanderthal bones was in a cave in Europe about 180 years ago. Since then, over 400 discoveries have been made.

Uncovering the Truth

Historians want to tell a story. They are curious about what really happened and how it happened. Just like detectives, historians must use evidence to solve history's mysteries. Check out these tools of the trade to learn how historians uncover the truth.

Interviewing eyewitnesses provides unique details about the event.

Many researchers reenact events to better understand how they might have happened.

Archaeologists dig for clues to find out more about how people lived in the past.

Historians analyze letters and journals that were written by people who watched historic events.

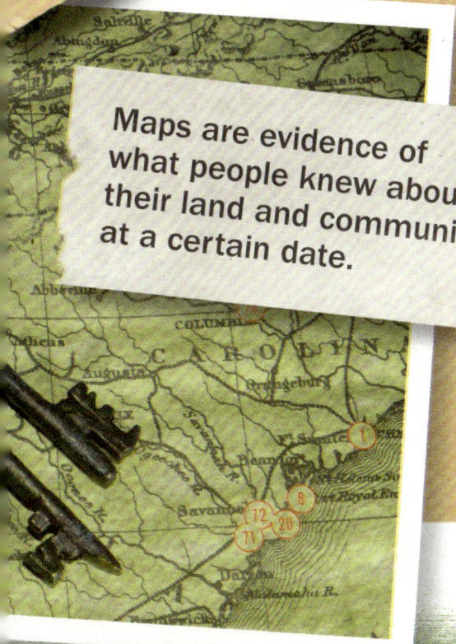

Maps are evidence of what people knew about their land and community at a certain date.

STOP! THINK...

- What tools do you think are most reliable?
- In what way do you think being a historian is different from being a detective?
- Which tools do you think would provide new information about the mysteries in this book?

Will We Ever Know?

Around the world and throughout history, things have happened that can't be explained. People may never know what happened or why. But that doesn't stop us from wondering. We want to know. And we won't stop looking until we figure it out . . . or die trying!

What events do **YOU** think historians might have gotten wrong?

Glossary

alibi—an excuse that shows a suspect was elsewhere at the time of a crime

allegedly—accused but without proof

Bastille—a French fortress that was used as a prison by French leaders for centuries

czar—a ruler of Russia until 1917

DNA tests—procedures used to identify someone or connect them to their ancestors

duchess—a royal title for a woman

extinct—no longer existing

Federal Bureau of Investigation (FBI)—an organization that investigates national crimes

genius—brilliance

hijacked—taken over by threat of death, especially a vehicle such as an airplane

hoax—a trick designed to get people to believe something is true when it is not

ransom—money paid to free people from hijackers or kidnappers

remains—anything that is left over or left behind

resources—materials and supplies that are highly needed or valuable

Teamsters—a trade union made up of people who drive trucks or wagons carrying cargo

traced—followed footprints or tracks

unions—groups of people who do the same type of work and join together to improve working conditions and pay

Index

Bibliography

Halls, Kelly Milner. *In Search of Sasquatch.* Houghton Mifflin Books for Children, 2011.

This book contains interviews with individuals ranging from expert scientists to everyday people who have claimed to see Sasquatch.

Mannis, Celeste Davidson. *Who Was William Shakespeare?* Grosset & Dunlap, 2006.

Learn about the mysterious life of William Shakespeare and his most famous works. Included in this book are diagrams of the Globe Theater, where many of his plays were performed.

Stewart, Robert, Clint Twist, and Edward Horton. *Mysteries of History.* National Geographic Society, 2003.

From the ancient Egyptian Pyramids to the Trojan horse, this book tells about mysteries in history from all over the world and all across time.

Tanaka, Shelley. *Amelia Earhart: The Legend of the Lost Aviator.* Abrams Books for Young Readers, 2008.

Beautiful illustrations, photographs, and interesting quotes tell the story of Amelia Earhart, the famous aviator. Her story is a mysterious and tragic one, and this book tells all about her career as a pilot and her disappearance.

Yolen, Jane, Heidi E.Y. Stemple, and Roger Roth. *Roanoke: The Lost Colony—An Unsolved Mystery from History.* Simon & Schuster Books for Young Readers, 2003.

Read about the mysterious disappearance of the Roanoke colony. Co-authored by a private detective, this book is filled with information on a mystery that has baffled people for centuries.

More to Explore

National Geographic

http://kids.nationalgeographic.com/kids/stories/history/salem-witch-trials/

This article provides information on the Salem Witch trials, written just for kids.

Kids Gen: Unsolved Mysteries

http://www.kidsgen.com/unsolved_mysteries/

Read about some historical mysteries that have eluded scientists. Topics include the Georgia Guidestones, the Loch Ness monster, the Bermuda Triangle, and the crystal skulls from the ancient Mayan and Incan ruins.

Myths and Legends

http://www.faqkids.com/myths-legends

These question-and-answer articles provide information on the Loch Ness monster and Bigfoot.

Kids Connect: Amelia Earhart

http://www.kidskonnect.com

From the home page, click on the *Subject Index*. Next, click on *People*, then click on *Earhart, Amelia*. Learn some basic facts about the life of Amelia Earhart, including her family and her educational background.

Encyclopedia Britannica for Kids

http://kids.britannica.com/

Encyclopedia Britannica Online provides a searchable database of information on any content you are studying in class or would like to know more about. Encyclopedia entries are written for kids ages 8–11 or 11 and up.

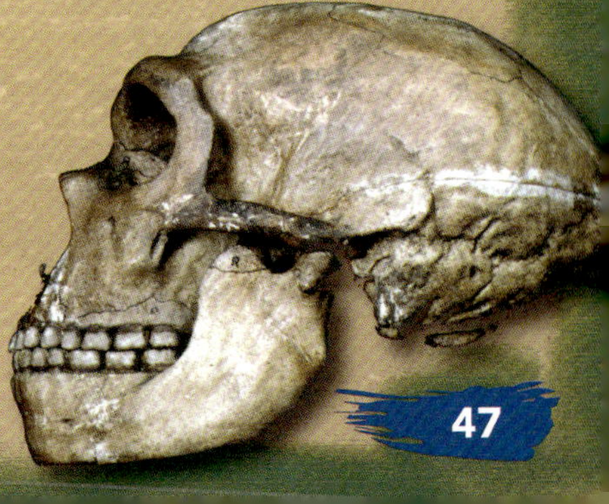

About the Author

Dona Herweck Rice grew up in Anaheim, California, and graduated from the University of Southern California with a degree in English and from the University of California at Berkeley with a credential for teaching. She has been a teacher in preschool through tenth grade, a researcher, a librarian, a theater director, and is now an editor, a poet, a writer of teacher materials, and a writer of books for children. She is married with two sons and lives in Southern California.